PACIFIC GLORY

PACIFIC GLORY

AIRLINES OF THE GREAT OCEAN

FREDDY BULLOCK

Airlife
England

Copyright © 1999 Freddy Bullock

First published in the UK in 1999
by Airlife Publishing Ltd

British Library Cataloguing-in-Publication Data
A catalogue record for this book
is available from the British Library

ISBN 1 85310 953 3

Typeset by Rowland Phototypesetting Ltd, Bury St Edmunds, Suffolk.
Printed in Hong Kong.

Airlife Publishing Ltd

101 Longden Road, Shrewsbury, SY3 9EB, England

Introduction

Pacific Glory attempts to cover the many airlines that fly across and within the confines of the world's largest ocean. From the Americas on its eastern flank, through the many small islands dotted across its waters, to the Asian rim on its western side, many of the world's international airlines are continually using this airspace every day.

In our ever shrinking world, tourism has probably been the greatest motivator for the vast increase in flying in this region. Many are attracted to the smaller Pacific islands, which in turn have created their own airlines, albeit small at the present time. Airlines like Polynesian, based in Western Samoa and Solomon Islands, operate only one Boeing 737 but provide an essential service.

A book of this nature always requires the help of other people and my thanks go first to my wife, Chris, for her unstinting support. I must also thank Captain Peter Thorpe and Julian Green of Qantas, Bob Donney and Kelly Meyer of Ansett, John Vogel, Ethel Pattison, Ricky-Dene Halliday of Aviation Data Centre, Reiner Geerdts and finally Rob Finlayson of Tasmania for all his help.

Producing this book has been pleasurable in many ways, not least the jump-seat trip into Hong Kong's Kai Tak airport aboard a Qantas Boeing 767, an experience not to be forgotten.

Freddy Bullock
England

ABOVE: This attractive colour scheme worn by Philippine Airlines Boeing 747-4F6 with an American registration, N752PR, shows the livery very well while it waits to commence its flight to Manila.

OPPOSITE ABOVE: The superb livery of Thai Airways' Boeing 747-4D7 HS-TGT is well illustrated in this picture as it turns on finals for landing in Hong Kong after its flight from Bangkok.

OPPOSITE BELOW: After landing in Hong Kong, Cathay Pacific Cargo's Boeing 747-467F, registered VR-HVK, taxies to the cargo unloading area.

BELOW: Air China Boeing 747-4J6 B-2466, is one of twelve such aircraft operated by the Chinese national airline on its international services around the world. Next in line for take-off on runway 13 at Kai Tak, this aircraft will shortly depart for Beijing.

OPPOSITE ABOVE: Vietnam Airlines aircraft are operated on their behalf by Region Air. This Boeing 767-324ER, registered S7-RGV, arrives in Hong Kong with a flight from Ho Chi Minh.

OPPOSITE BELOW: Malaysia Airlines lease several MD-11s from the American airline World Airways. This example, N271WA, has arrived from Kuala Lumpur and is seen taxying to its gate for unloading.

BELOW: China Xinhua's Boeing 737-341, B-2908, sits on the ramp in Beijing between flights. This company flies out of Urumqi in the Xiajiang province. (*RF*)

OPPOSITE BELOW: Based in the Solomon Islands, Pacific Air Express operate one Boeing 727-281F, registered H4-PAE, which is seen here at Sydney Kingsford-Smith airport awaiting its next load of freight. (*RF*)

OPPOSITE ABOVE: Delta's MD-11 rests between flights at Los Angeles. This type is used to fly the routes across the Pacific to Tokyo and Seoul.

BELOW: Proud owners of this 500th Beech 1900 series aircraft, Impulse Airlines painted D-model VH-TRW in a special scheme to highlight the event. It is used on services to and from Sydney Mascot Airport. (*RF*)

OPPOSITE ABOVE: In this very striking livery Orient Express' Boeing 727-225, HS-PTB, taxies for take-off from Bangkok with a flight to Chiang Mai, its home base. (*RF*)

OPPOSITE BELOW: After arriving from Taipei with flight GE 593 TransAsia's A320-231, registered B-22301, taxies to the terminal in Macau. (*RF*)

BELOW: Japan Air's Boeing 747-246B, registered JA 8125, slowly taxies to the threshold of runway 13 at Hong Kong's Kai Tak airport in preparation for take-off on its flight to Tokyo.

OPPOSITE ABOVE: The world's largest parcels carrier, based in Memphis, Tennessee, is FedEx (Federal Express). They fly regular services across the Pacific. MD-11 N886FE arrives in Hong Kong via Japan with a scheduled flight from Memphis.

OPPOSITE BELOW: Cathay Pacific's A330-342 VR-HLJ is illustrated turning onto runway 13 in Hong Kong, prior to take-off.

ABOVE: Philippine Airlines have twelve Airbus A300s in their fleet. Bearing a French registration, F-OHPC is about to land in Hong Kong after a flight from Manila.

OPPOSITE ABOVE: Boeing 757-21B B-2804 is another example of China Southern's expanding fleet of Western-built aircraft. This flight from Guangzhou is about to land in Hong Kong.

OPPOSITE BELOW: Thai Airlines' new Airbus A330-322s now operate many services previously flown by Airbus A300s on routes in the Far East and Pacific rim. This example, registered HS-TED, is ready to depart from Hong Kong for Bangkok.

BELOW: LanChile's Boeing 767-375ER CC-CRH waits for its next load of passengers at Los Angeles before its flight home to Santiago.

OPPOSITE BELOW: Mount Cook Airlines have for many years flown the HS 748. On a flight from Christchurch to Mount Cook and Queenstown, ZK-MCF diverted to a small strip at Pukaki due to bad weather in Mount Cook, before flying onto its final destination.

OPPOSITE ABOVE: This BAe 146-200, registered ZK-NZA, and flown by Ansett New Zealand has just arrived in Christchurch on the South Island with a flight from Queenstown.

BELOW: Kunming in south-east China is the base for Yunnan Airlines. Their Boeing 737-3Y0, registered B-2539, is in push-back mode from its gate at Beijing Airport prior to flying back to its home base. (*RF*)

ABOVE: Mandala, an Indonesian airline, fly scheduled services, mainly on the island of Java. Boeing 737-2V5 PK-RIK waits in Jakarta for its next flight. (*RF*)

ABOVE: Canadian Airlines' flight CP 7, a non-stop service from Vancouver, turns for final approach to Hong Kong with Boeing 747-475 C-FBCA in charge.

OPPOSITE ABOVE: China Northern's DC-9-82, B-2138, arrives in Hong Kong after a flight from Shenyang in Northern China.

OPPOSITE BELOW: Dragonair, a wholly owned subsidiary of Cathay Pacific, operate a fleet of Airbus A320s and A330s from their Hong Kong base. The airline was originally created to fly charters but now flies many scheduled flights, mostly to mainland China. This example, A320 VR-HYU, is preparing for take-off.

BELOW: Air Nauru's sole aircraft is Boeing 737-4L7 C2-RN10, which flies to many destinations within the Pacific. It is seen here at Guam's Agana Airport after a flight from its home base. (*ADC*)

OPPOSITE ABOVE: United Airlines now fly four DC-10-30CFs under the title of Worldwide Cargo. N1859U is illustrated on the ramp at Osaka Kansai. (*ADC*)

OPPOSITE BELOW: One of many small operators within the Philippines is DHC-7 RP-C2988 owned by Asian Spirit and seen here in Manila. (*ADC*)

BELOW: Air Calédonie's Twin Otter, F-ODGI, is parked at Noumea between its inter-island flights. (RG).

OPPOSITE ABOVE: Christchurch on the South Island of New Zealand is the scene for Fieldair's DC-3 ZK-AMR as it taxies to the cargo area for unloading.

OPPOSITE BELOW: Based in Papeete on the beautiful island of Tahiti, operating with a fleet of ATR 42s and 72s, Air Tahiti is the major airline servicing the surrounding islands. This illustration shows ATR 72-202 F-OHAG on the ground at its base airport. (*RG*)

BELOW: HS-TME, an MD-11 of Thai Airlines, is now lined up on the centre-line to land in Hong Kong after its flight from Bangkok.

ABOVE: The imposing front-end of Canadian Airlines' Boeing 747-475 C-FGHZ in flight.

BELOW: Bouraq Indonesia Airlines still use their dwindling fleet of HS 748s on local flights. PK-IHG is shown here at Denpasar. (*ADC*)

OPPOSITE ABOVE: Still giving service after over 40 years is this Douglas C-47B of Mabuhay Airlines, which is one of two used by the airline out of Manila. (*ADC*)

OPPOSITE BELOW: This Royal Tongan HS 748, V7-8203, was on lease from Air Marshall Island Airways when this photograph was taken. (*ADC*)

BELOW: Still wearing the old style livery of China Airlines, Airbus A300 B-1812 nears the end of flight CI 609 from the Taiwanese capital, Taipei.

OPPOSITE ABOVE: Japan Air's daily flight JL 705 from Nagoya is flown by DC-10s or MD11s. On this occasion DC-10-40 JA 8541 was flying the service and is about to land in Hong Kong.

OPPOSITE BELOW: The daily flight from Tokyo Narita Airport flown by All Nippon operates under the code NH 909. Boeing 747-2D3B JA8192 was flying the service to Hong Kong on 26 December 1996.

BELOW: Japan Air Cargo operate their Boeing 747 freighters in this modern 'Super Logistics' scheme, which looks very impressive. Bearing an American registration, N211JL these aircraft are used extensively on Pacific routes.

OPPOSITE ABOVE: Korean Air's flight KE617 will soon be landing in Hong Kong after the non-stop flight from the Korean capital. Airbus A300 HL-7298 is in charge.

OPPOSITE BELOW: The imposing front-end of China Airlines Boeing 747-209B B-1866 is well illustrated as it waits for take-off on its flight to Taipei.

ABOVE: After loading with passengers Thai Airways' Boeing 747-2D7B HS-TGG taxies for take-off from Sydney Kingsford-Smith with flight TG 992, non-stop to Bangkok.

ABOVE: Qantas still fly two Boeing 747SP aircraft, mainly on the route to Taipei. VH-EAA is inside the maintenance hangar at Sydney Airport receiving attention.

ABOVE: Air New Zealand's new colour scheme stands out well on the front-end of Boeing 747-419 ZK-NBT.

LEFT: The tails of Air New Zealand's Boeing 747 and Boeing 767 stand out in the evening sun at Sydney's Kingsford-Smith Airport.

BELOW: Solomon Airlines' sole Boeing 737-376, VH-TJB, is operated by Qantas on their behalf. Flights from Honiara to Sydney are made via Melbourne, a long trip for a Boeing 737.

OPPOSITE ABOVE: On a beautiful morning in Sydney, Qantas' Boeing 737-476 VH-TJS taxies to the terminal after landing with a domestic flight.

OPPOSITE BELOW: Hazelton Air Services are a small commuter operator flying within the state of New South Wales. Saab 340B VH-TCH taxies for take-off.

ABOVE: Based at Nadi in Fiji, Air Pacific is the national carrier flying to many points within the Pacific. This Boeing 767-300 series aircraft, registered DQ-FJC, has just been pushed back ready for departure from Sydney's Kingsford-Smith airport with flight FJ 914 to Nadi.

OPPOSITE ABOVE: Eastern Australia, a subsidiary of Qantas, fly the shorter domestic routes within the state of New South Wales. DHC-8 VH-TQG waits on the ramp for its next turn of duty.

OPPOSITE BELOW: Impulse Airlines now use an all-Beech 1900D fleet of aircraft on their short-haul services out of Sydney's Mascot Airport. VH-SMH has just loaded with passengers and is ready for clearance to depart for Coma, New South Wales.

BELOW: Another major American parcels carrier with scheduled services across the Pacific is United Parcel Services or UPS for short. N683UP is an older Boeing 747-121 series originally operated by Pan Am.

OPPOSITE ABOVE: China Eastern's A300B4-605R, B-2321, flies frequent scheduled services from Shanghai to Hong Kong.

OPPOSITE BELOW: Japan Air now use some of their Boeing 747-246Bs under the marketing title of 'Super Resort Express'. They are painted in an attractive holiday scheme. JA8110 taxies away from the terminal in Sydney, prior to departure to Tokyo.

BELOW: Of interest to the 'plane spotter', Boeing 767-204ER VH-RMO, belonging to Ansett, was originally flown by the British charter operator Britannia under the registration G-BNCW.

OPPOSITE ABOVE: A subsidiary of Ansett, Aero Pelican fly four DHC-6 Twin Otters on local services out of Kingsford-Smith. VH-KZQ taxies for take-off.

OPPOSITE BELOW: China Eastern now use their Airbus A340s on services between Beijing and Sydney. B-2380 touches down in Australia after its overnight flight from the Chinese capital.

OPPOSITE ABOVE: Qantas' A300B4 VH-TAD climbs out of Sydney into a beautiful sky on a delightful January morning in 1997.

OPPOSITE BELOW: Tamair's Swearingen Metro looks very attractive in its red and gold livery, after arriving in Sydney with a flight from Tamworth, New South Wales.

BELOW: An imposing picture of a Thai Boeing 747-3D7, HS-TGE, as it taxies past the photographer on its way for take-off.

BELOW: An Ansett Boeing 737-33A, registered VH-CZT, is seen here as it taxies to the terminal at Kingsford-Smith in Sydney.

OPPOSITE ABOVE: The clean lines of Air New Zealand's new corporate livery are clearly seen on Boeing 767-219ER ZK-NBC at Melbourne Tullamarine Airport.

OPPOSITE BELOW: Qantas Airlink's British Aerospace BAe 146-100 series VH-NJR arrives in Adelaide after a flight from Kalgoorlie. These aircraft are flown by National Jet.

ABOVE: Polynesian Airlines, based in Apia, Western Samoa, operate one jet aircraft – namely this Boeing 737-3Q8, registered 5W-ILF. Flight PH 832 to Apia via Wellington in New Zealand sits at the gate in Melbourne.

LEFT: The colourful tail of Polynesian's Boeing 737-3Q8.

BELOW: Malaysia Airlines' Boeing 737-5H6 9M-MFG sits in the hot midday sun at Singapore's Changi Airport while it waits for passengers to board prior to the flight to Kuala Lumpur.

OPPOSITE ABOVE: China Eastern's A300B4 B-2319 is being pushed from the gate at Singapore Changi Airport. MU 546 is a non-stop flight to Shanghai.

OPPOSITE BELOW: Thai Airlines' latest Boeing product, the B-777, is now in service with the airline and extensively used in the Pacific/Asia rim. HS-TJA sits at the gate at Singapore Changi airport.

BELOW: Singapore Airlines have seventeen Airbus A310-324s in their fleet and 9V-STC is seen in push-back mode at Singapore Changi Airport.

OPPOSITE ABOVE: Myanmar Airways International fly four Boeing 737-400 series aircraft from their base in Yangon. This example, TC-AYA, was leased from Istanbul Airlines of Turkey for a short period and is seen in Singapore prior to its flight back to Yangon. It has since been returned to its owners.

OPPOSITE BELOW: The front-end of Asiana's Boeing 747-48E, registered HL-7418.

BELOW: For a short period Qantas flew their two Boeing 747SPs in the livery of Australia Asia. VH-EAA has just arrived in Los Angeles with a flight from Sydney. These aircraft have now been repainted in Qantas colours.

OPPOSITE ABOVE: Aloha Airlines, based in Honolulu, fly only domestic services between the Hawaiian islands and use the Boeing 737. N803AL is a 200 series.

OPPOSITE BELOW: Rarotonga is the main island within the Cook Islands. Air Rarotonga fly two EMB Bandeirantes with ZK-FTS being shown in this picture.

ABOVE: Malaysia Airlines' MD-11 N273WA, which is leased from World Airways of the United States, arrives in Hong Kong with flight MH72 from Kuala Lumpur.

OPPOSITE ABOVE: Japan Asia, a subsidiary company of Japan Air, was created for the sole purpose of flying to Taiwan. DC-10-40 JA 8532 is shown on finals to Hong Kong on flight EG 205 from Tokyo Narita and Taipei.

OPPOSITE BELOW: Very few of the world's airlines now fly the Boeing 747SP. However, Korean Air still operate two examples, one of which, HL-7457, is illustrated here awaiting departure with a flight from Hong Kong to Seoul.

BELOW: Hawaiian Air DC-10-10s are used on the route from Honolulu to Los Angeles. Having arrived in LA, N162AA taxies to the arrivals gate.

OPPOSITE ABOVE: Jal Cargo's 'Super Logistics' Boeing 747-246F has finished loading and awaits instructions to proceed to taxi and take-off from Los Angeles with its flight back to Japan. Out of six freighters operated, this aircraft is the only one in an all-metal finish.

OPPOSITE BELOW: Air Pacific's sole Boeing 747-238B, registered DQ-FJE and leased from Qantas, gathers speed down runway 12L at Los Angeles and in seconds will lift-off with flight FJ811 at the start of its non-stop flight to Nadi.

ABOVE: The colourful tail section of a
Philippine Airlines' MD-11ER.

OPPOSITE ABOVE: A long way from its
Pacific base in Manila is this Philippine
Airlines A340-211 bearing a French
registration, F-OHPJ. It is lined up
perfectly for landing at London Heathrow
at the completion of its flight.

OPPOSITE BELOW: The impressive front-end
of All Nippon's Boeing 747-481 JA8962.

BELOW: With seconds to go before landing in Los Angeles, this EVA Air Boeing 747-45E, registered B-16462, nears the completion of flight BR 12 from Taipei.

OPPOSITE ABOVE: VP 897 is the flight number of the Brazilian carrier VASP. Having arrived earlier from Seoul, MD-11 PP-SPE is pushed back ready for the continuing sectors to São Paulo and Rio de Janeiro from Los Angeles.

OPPOSITE BELOW: American Trans Air modified the livery on their TriStar 50, N180AT, to Pleasant Hawaiian Holidays for use mainly on this very busy holiday route.

BELOW: Nippon Cargo Airlines operate a fleet of eight Boeing 747 cargo aircraft which regularly fly across the Pacific to the United States and other destinations, including Hong Kong. JA 8191 is ready to depart the latter airport for its flight back to Japan.

OPPOSITE ABOVE: Over the last ten years many new airlines have been created in China, mostly using Western-built aircraft. China Eastern, based in Shanghai, is such an airline as this photograph illustrates with their DC-9-82, registered B-2127.

OPPOSITE BELOW: China Airlines Boeing 747-409 B-161 shows off the company's new livery as it lands in Hong Kong after its flight from Taipei.

BELOW: The front-end of Dragonair's A330-342, VR-HLB, highlights the airline's clean-cut image.

OPPOSITE ABOVE: Formerly known as CAAC, the state-run airline is now operated as Air China. This Boeing 737-3J6, registered B-2953, is one of fifteen flown by the company.

OPPOSITE BELOW: Asiana's flight OZ 301 (non-stop from the South Korean capital, Seoul) is about to land in Hong Kong, with Boeing 767-38EER HL 7263 in charge.

BELOW: On finals for landing in Sydney is this Qantas Boeing 747-338, registered VH-EBU, painted in a dramatic aboriginal colour scheme, which is entitled 'Nalanji Dreaming'. (*RF*)

OPPOSITE ABOVE: In the process of being pushed-back from the gate at Melbourne's Tullamarine Airport, this Merpati A310-324, registered PK-MAX, is in the first stage of commencing its flight back to Indonesia. This aircraft is named after the 8th century Buddhist temple 'Boroburdur'. (*RF*)

OPPOSITE BELOW: New Caledonia is a French Protectorate lying north of the Tropic of Capricorn and due west of Queensland. Aircalin use this one Boeing 737-33A, F-ODGX, which is seen in Sydney preparing for flight SB 161 to Brisbane and Noumea. (*RF*)

BELOW: Asiana's Boeing 737-48E HL-7509 looks superb as it taxies to the gate in Macau after a flight from the South Korean capital, Seoul. (*RF*)

OPPOSITE ABOVE: To celebrate 50 years of flying (1947–1997) Singapore Airlines painted Boeing 777-212 9V-SQA in a special scheme. It was photographed at Changi Airport. (*RF*)

OPPOSITE BELOW: Silk Air, based at Singapore's Changi Airport, fly two Fokker 100s and six Boeing 737-300s to various destinations in Malaya and Thailand. 9V-TRE is the 300 series illustrated here. (*RF*)

LEFT: Macau is still administered by Portugal and the relatively new airline Air Macau is expanding quickly. A321-131 CS-MAF taxies for take-off from Bangkok for the flight back to its base. (*RF*)

ABOVE: One can almost see the passengers in this bird's-eye view of Dragonair's A320 VR-HYO on approach to Kai Tak.

BELOW: Singapore Airlines are well known for operating a modern fleet of aircraft. 9V-SMN is one of forty Boeing 747-412s flown around the world by the company. The flight illustrated is a Singapore–Hong Kong–Taipei service operated on a daily basis.

ABOVE: Shenzhen Airlines, from the province of Guangdon, used Boeing 737-3K9 B-2933 on its service to Beijing. (*RF*)

OPPOSITE ABOVE: Thai Airbus' A330-322 HS-TEC looks very striking in this picture taken at Singapore Changi Airport. (*RF*)

OPPOSITE BELOW: Another growing Indonesian airline is Sempati. Boeing 737-281 PK-JHF is seen here at Jakarta. (*RF*)

BELOW: Air Great Wall, based in Sichuan, still use the rather old Tu-154M on their charter services. B-2628 will shortly depart from Beijing. (*RF*)

OPPOSITE ABOVE: China Southwest, from Chengdu in the province of Sichuan, were using Boeing 737-3Z0 B-2597 when this picture was taken in Beijing. (*RF*)

OPPOSITE BELOW: Air Pacific operate Boeing 737-33A DQ-FJD on behalf of Royal Tongan. After operating a flight from Tonga the aircraft is seen at Nadi in Fiji. (*RF*)

ABOVE: Pacific East Asia Cargo of the Philippines operate two of their BAe 146 200QTs on behalf of TNT. RP-C481 is the aircraft shown here. (*ADC*)

BELOW: To highlight the Olympic Games being held in Sydney in the year 2000, Ansett are painting some of their aircraft in a special scheme. A320 VH-HYB was the first to be painted and is seen just on take-off from Kingsford-Smith Airport. (*JV*)

BELOW: To celebrate 50 years of flying the Pacific, Northwest Airlines specially painted Boeing 747-451 N670US in this delightful World Plane Scheme. The location is Tokyo Narita Airport. (*ADC*)

OPPOSITE ABOVE: LBC Airways, a small Philippines operator based in Manila use two HS 748s for their services, one of which, RP-C1017, is shown here. (*RF*)

OPPOSITE BELOW: Waiting for its next flight, Aboitiz Air Transport's NAMC YS 11A, registered RP-C3202, sits on the ramp in Manila. (*RF*)

LEFT: When this photograph was taken Air Philippines were leasing this Boeing 737-266 from Air Atlanta of Iceland, hence the TF-ABG registration. (*ADC*)

OPPOSITE ABOVE: Fokker 100 B-2239 of China Eastern arrives on finals to Hong Kong's Kai Tak airport after a flight from Ningbo in mainland China.

OPPOSITE BELOW: Air China's Boeing 767-3J6ER, registered B-2558, comes to the threshold of runway 13 at Hong Kong Kai Tak as it becomes number one for take-off.

ABOVE: A striking front-end picture of a Thai MD-11, prior to landing.

BELOW: Northwest Cargo have been flying their Boeing 747-251F freighters across the Pacific for over twenty years. N616US is one of four original aircraft delivered as pure freighters in 1976.

OPPOSITE ABOVE: After being stored for a period, Garuda's Airbus A300 PK-GAK was placed back in service wearing an all-white scheme with blue titles. It is seen on finals here at Hong Kong on a flight from Denpasar, Bali.

OPPOSITE BELOW: In terms of passengers carried, China Southern based in the province of Guangzhou, are now the largest airline in China and still expanding rapidly. Their Boeing 737-31B, registered B-2596, is about to depart Hong Kong on a flight back to its home base.

BELOW: Japan Air System, or JAS for short,
is a large Japanese domestic carrier based
in Tokyo. DC-9-87 JA 8278 is one of many
McDonnell Douglas aircraft used by the
company and is seen at Osaka Itami
Airport. (ADC)

OPPOSITE ABOVE: Air Ad's solitary HS 748,
RP-C1023, rests between flights in Manila.
(ADC)

OPPOSITE BELOW: Boeing 737-230 PK-MBC,
flown by Merpati, arrives in Denpasar on
the island of Bali after a flight from the
mainland of Java. (ADC)

OPPOSITE ABOVE: With the introduction of the new MD-90-30s Japan Air System created a stylish modern livery as shown on JA 8062, waiting for departure from Osaka Kansai. (*ADC*)

OPPOSITE BELOW: Hawaiian Air's DC-9-51, registered N679HA, prepares to leave Honolulu on another inter-island flight. (*ADC*)

BELOW: After its long flight from Nadi in Fiji, Air Pacific's Boeing 767-3X2ER, registered DQ-FJC, taxies to the gate at Narita International Airport, Tokyo. (*ADC*)

OPPOSITE ABOVE: Osaka Kansai is an airport built on reclaimed land for the 21st century and is an outstanding engineering feat with connections to the mainland by road and rail. Japan Air System's DC-9-81, registered JA 8296, will shortly depart on a domestic flight. (*ADC*)

OPPOSITE BELOW: No longer in business, Adona Aviation used this A310 200 series, registered VR-BQU, which is seen here in Penang, Malaysia. (*ADC*)

ABOVE: Aloha Island Air, a subsidiary of
Aloha Air, use their DHC-6s on short haul
flights within the Hawaiian islands.
N705PV is seen at Honolulu. The company
has now changed its name to Island Air.
(*RF*)

ABOVE: This Cook Island Air DHC-6, ZK-KHA, has just arrived in Rarotonga and the baggage handlers are already waiting to unload.

BELOW: Grand Air is a relatively new airline operator with a fleet of one Airbus A300 and four Boeing 737-200s. When this picture was taken the aircraft carried a French registration number, F-OHPN, and was operating a service to Manila. (*RG*)

OPPOSITE ABOVE: Based on the aboriginal art of the Yanyuwa people and entitled 'Wunala Dreaming' (Kangaroo Dreaming) this Qantas Boeing 747-438, VH-OJB, certainly looks very colourful as it taxies for take-off in Sydney. (*RF*)

OPPOSITE BELOW: With engines running this Air Nelson SA.227SC Metro 111 prepares to depart from Christchurch on the South Island of New Zealand with a local commuter flight.

BELOW: Flight AE 801 from Taipei touches down at Sydney Kingsford-Smith Airport. This services is flown exclusively by Mandarin Airlines' Boeing 747SPs. The example illustrated is B-1880.

OPPOSITE ABOVE: A Singapore Airlines 'MEGA ARK' Boeing 747-412F, registered 9V-SFC, having arrived in Sydney with a flight from Singapore taxies past the International Terminal to the cargo area for unloading.

OPPOSITE BELOW: A Boeing 737-377 VH-CZG of Ansett has just departed the gate at Sydney's Kingsford-Smith domestic terminal, ready for another inter-Australian flight.

ABOVE: Continental Micronesia, the Pacific arm of its American parent company Continental Airlines, is based in Saipan on the Marianas Islands, which form part of a US Trust Territory in the eastern Pacific. DC-10-10 N68041 touches down in Sydney, where the engines are put into reverse thrust to assist with braking. (*RF*)

ABOVE: Flying inter-regional services within Thailand, Bangkok Air use the ATR 72 on their flights as this picture of HS-PGD shows. (*RF*)

BELOW: A DC9-82 of U-Land Airlines prepares to land at Taipei Sung Shan Airport with a domestic flight. (*RF*)

OPPOSITE ABOVE: Another Taiwanese airline is Uni-Air which flies mostly domestic services. An MD-90-30 is illustrated landing at Kaohsiung. (*RF*)

OPPOSITE BELOW: Separate from the international airport, Taipei's Sung Shan primarily caters for domestic flights. Far Eastern Air Transport's Boeing 757-2Q8, registered B-27005, looks very striking sitting on the ramp. (*RF*)

BELOW: Japan Air System have recently introduced a varied new colour scheme for their fleet. This MD-90-30, registered JA-8064, shows one example taxying at Tokyo Haneda Airport. (*RF*)

OPPOSITE ABOVE: Bouraq Indonesian Airlines have been flying for many years within their own country. Boeing 737-2H6 PK-IJE is shown taxying at Jakarta. (*RF*)

OPPOSITE BELOW: Japan TransOcean Air are based in Naha, Okinawa, which forms part of the Ryukyu Islands some 300 miles southeast of mainland Japan. Boeing 737-2Q3 JA 8250 waits on the ramp in Naha for its next flight. (*RF*)

BELOW: Based in Xian City, Shaanxi Province, China Northwest were using A310-222 registered B-2301, when this picture was taken in Hong Kong. (*RF*)